Granados masterpieces

12 danzas espanolas

(Spanish Dances)

A CONTEMPORARY MASTERPIECE ALBUM

CONTENTS

Published 1941 by Edward B. Marks Music Company
International Copyright Secured   Made in U.S.A.   All Rights Reserved

EDWARD B. MARKS MUSIC COMPANY

EXCLUSIVELY DISTRIBUTED BY HAL•LEONARD CORPORATION
7777 W. BLUEMOUND RD. P.O. BOX 13819 MILWAUKEE, WI 53213

T0050951

12 DANZAS ESPANOLAS
1
Minueto

Edited by Luis Sucra

By E. Granados, op. 5

Published 1941 by Edward B. Marks Music Company

2
ORIENTAL

Edited by Luis Sucra

By E. Granados, op. 5

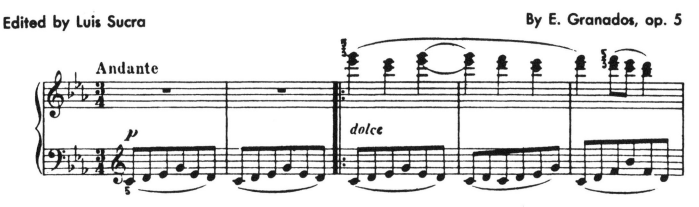

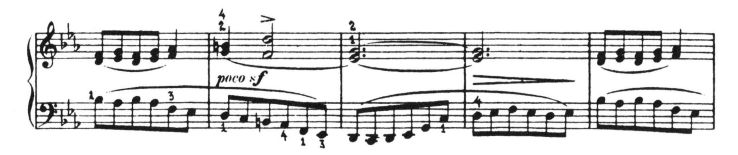

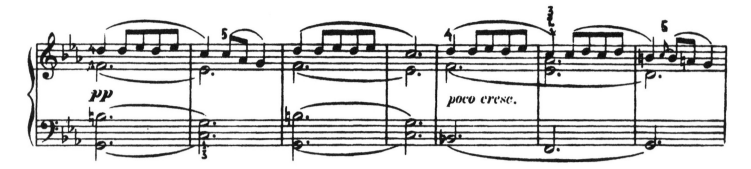

3
ZARABANDA

Edited by Luis Sucra

By E. Granados, op. 5

Allegro maestoso.

4
VILLANESCA

Edited by Luis Sucra

By E. Granados, op. 5

Andante espress. *a tempo*

Andante espress.

Cancion y estribillo.

Molto andante.

Andante espress.   *a tempo*

Andante espress.

rit. molto e dim.   *pp*

5
ANDALUZA (Playera)

Edited by Luis Sucra

By E. Granados, op. 5

Andantino quasi Allegretto

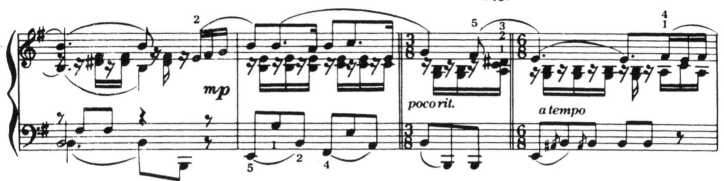

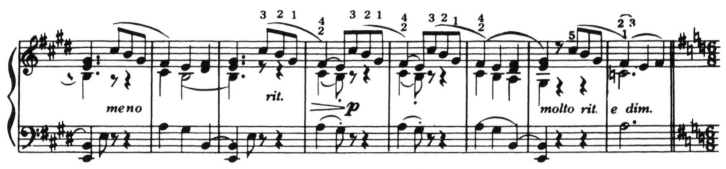

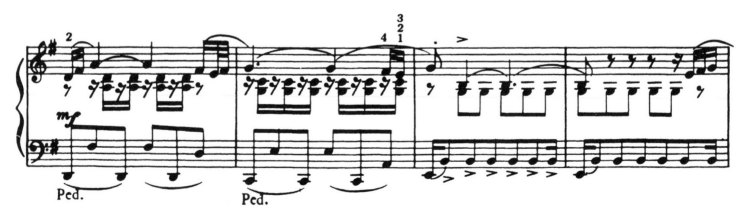

6
JOTA (Rondalla Aragonesa)

Edited by Luis Sucra

By E. Granados, op. 5

Allegretto, poco a poco accelerando.

Molto andante, espressivo.

Tempo I.

poco a poco cresc.

p

poco più f

sempre accel. e cresc.

cresc. sempre e animando molto

sempre più ff e accel.

7
VALENCIANA

Edited by Luis Sucra

By E. Granados, op. 5

Poco più mosso.

dim. molto e rit.   *poco rit.*   *stacc.*

Tempo I.

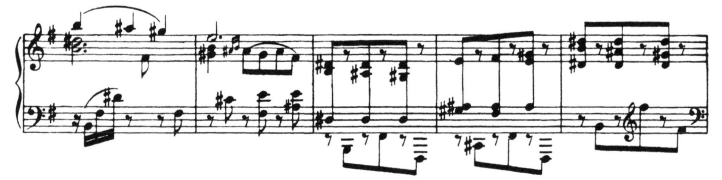

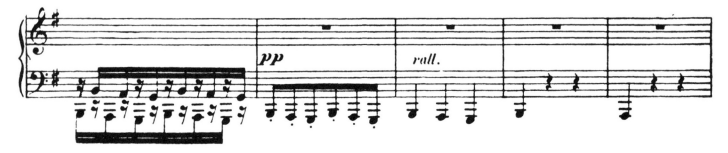

8
ASTURIANA

Edited by Luis Sucra

By E. Granados, op. 5

Moderato assai.

con pedale

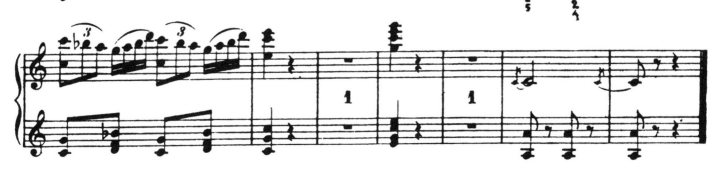

9
MAZURCA

Edited by Luis Sucra

By E. Granados, op. 5

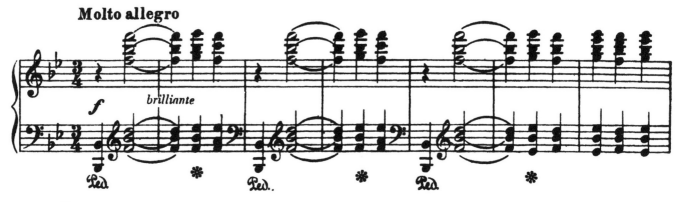

10
DANZA TRISTE

Edited by Luis Sucra

By E. Granados, op. 5

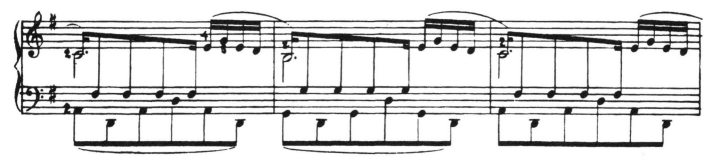

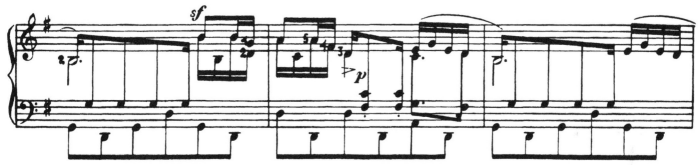

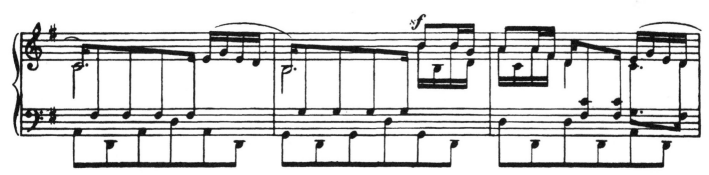

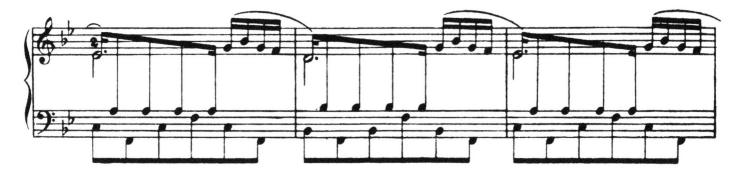

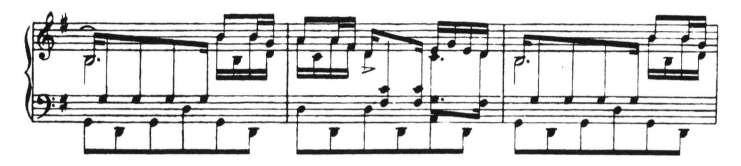

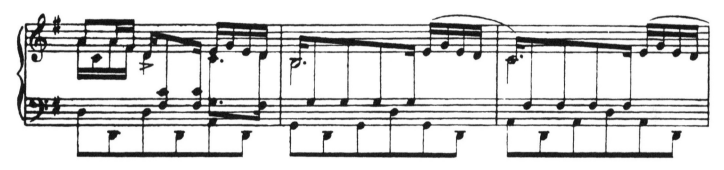

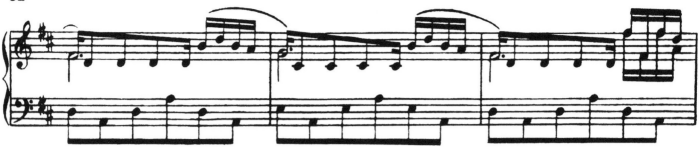

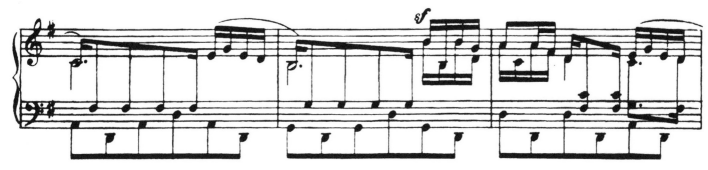

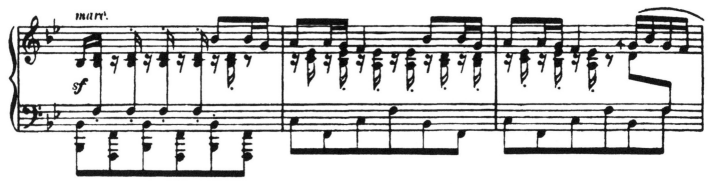

11
ZAMBRA

Edited by Luis Sucra

By E. Granados, op. 5

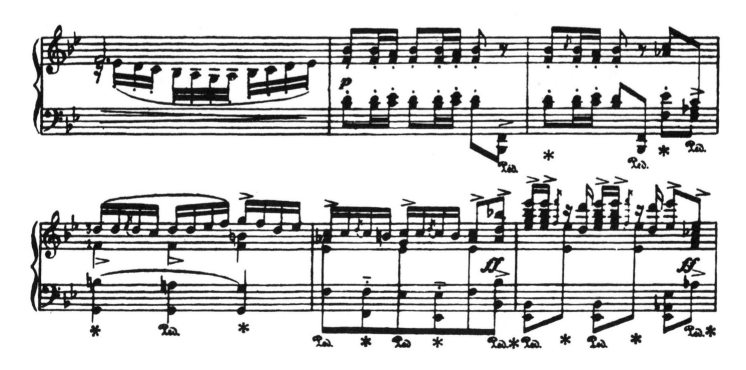

60

12
ARABESCA

Edited by Luis Sucra

By E. Granados, op. 5

Tempo I.

poco a poco

rall. e dim.

Molto andante espressivo

marcato il canto

dolce

dim.

rit molto

Andante.

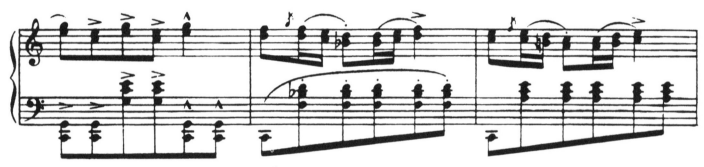